Is It

Liam Darcy Books

.

In 2024 an author was arrested for stirring up racial hatred and promoting anti-immigrant feeling. This is the story about his arrest and what prompted it, and it's dedicated to all those who supported him. Many thanks to Billy Graham.

You Wait Eight Days For A Copper To Come And Then Five Turn Up At Once

What would you consider the more serious offence; a house burglary in a working class area or a flyer promoting a book being put through the letter box of a house in an upper class area?

The answer, obviously, is a house burglary in a working class area. Though Greater Manchester Police think differently.

And out of those two 'offences' - the latter of which 99.9% of people *wouldn't* class as an offence - which do you think requires a more speedy response by the police? Again, the house burglary is the answer.

But yet again Greater Manchester Police think differently. They think that a flyer being posted through the letter box of a house in an upper class area warrants a more speedy response.

Within 24 hours to be exact.

I recently released a revised edition of a previous book I did and out of courtesy I contacted all those whose stories are in the book to tell them I was doing so. Some replied some didn't.

One of those who did reply was a fella called Joe who lives in Sheffield. His story was titled Dear Jeremy Corbyn, Jo Swinson, Gina Miller, Tony Blair And The Like. It was about Brexit and how people tried to overturn the result and stop Brexit from happening.

Joe voted leave. And in his story, or letter as he called it, he talks about illegal immigrants flocking to the UK, which was the main reason people voted to leave the EU.

Joe asked me if he could add a few things to his story so I said yes and told him to email them to me and I'd stick them in for him. He also asked if he could change the title of his story. So I said yes, no problem, and asked him what he wanted it changing to. And he said, "I want to change it to 'The More Illegal Immigrants That Drown In The Channel The Better – People Are Sick To Death Of Them Coming Here."

I thought, "Fuck Me! That's a bit strong!" I'm sick to death of them coming here too, like most people are, but I wouldn't wish for them to drown in the English Channel. Send them to Rwanda when they get here by all means but it's a bit much wishing for them to drown trying to get here.

And so I suggested to Joe that he keep the same title or use a different one but he was adamant he wanted that one. So I thought 'well it's his story and if that's what he wants to call it it's his choice.'

Not far from where I live is a place called Hale, in Cheshire. It's a very posh area and there were plans to house over a hundred asylum seekers in a hotel in the centre of the village which the locals weren't too happy about.

And the government have since moved more asylum seekers into another hotel just up the road in Altrincham, the Cresta Court.

However unlike the hotel in Hale where notice was given to residents about the proposal to move asylum seekers in, notice wasn't given to locals in Altrincham and they just shut the hotel with immediate effect one morning.

Not surprisingly residents of Altrincham were highly pissed off about it. So too were those who had booked to stay at the hotel and those who had booked parties, their wedding reception, and other functions there.

Local business owners such as restaurants, eateries, shops, bars, pubs etc were annoyed too. And it's *no wonder* they were annoyed. They've lost a lot of income, because hotel residents would go out and spend money with them. The hotel used to have coach loads of Manchester United fans coming over from Ireland every week or whenever United were playing at home and they'd spend a lot of money visiting the bars, restaurants etc, and over the course of the football season they'd spend tens of thousands of pounds in the local area.

But that's now gone. And local business owners are tens of thousands of pounds down.

Apparently, it even affected the housing market around the area. And by all accounts one resident who lived near the hotel lost the sale of their house after the purchasers found out about the asylum seekers moving in and pulled out of the sale.

Now even though I thought Joe's new title was a bit harsh, from a publicity point of view it was gold. It's an attention grabber. So I had over two and a half thousand flyers printed and used his story, along with the title of it, to publicise my book.

And that's the ONLY reason I used it - to publicise the book. And I posted the flyers around Hale.

As I was posting the leaflets quite a few people stopped me and asked about the book saying it looked very interesting and that they were going to buy it. They were very friendly and polite and I stood and chatted with some of them for a few minutes.

However someone else stopped me too, an elderly woman. Though she wasn't friendly or polite. She was fucking rude and ill-mannered.

She'd come out of a house on a road called Westgate and she was the passenger in a car and she had one of the flyer's in her hand and she wound the window down and said, "It's disgusting wishing people should drown. You shouldn't be putting these through people's letter boxes. I'm going to the police."

So I said to her, "Hang on a minute. Let me explain. It's not my story. I only published the book..." But as I was talking she wound the car window up and motioned to me with her hand in a 'shooing' fashion to go away. So I motioned back to her with *my hand* for her to wind the window down and mouthed, "Put your window down please - I'll explain."

In hindsight I should've just motioned with two fingers telling her to fuck off!

She *did* wind her window down, very briefly. But as I started to talk she interrupted me and cut me off. And in a raised voice she said, "I'm NOT interested. Go away. You're disgusting. I'm going to the police with this," and shooed me away with her hand again and wound the window up and they drove off.

I thought, "Oh fuck off you stupid stuck up bitch!" (and the bloke that was driving was a prick too, wittering on with himself) and I didn't think any more of it and carried on posting the flyers.

I wasn't bothered in the slightest about her going to the police because in my eyes I hadn't done anything wrong. All I'd done was use parts of a story - a story that wasn't mine - to promote my book. Albeit the story had a title that I suppose you could describe as controversial. But I'd even put on the flyer that some people may find the title of Joe's story distasteful.

However even though *I* thought I hadn't done anything wrong, the police thought differently and the following day at around half eight on a Sunday morning nearly half a dozen coppers turned up at my house in two cars and a police van and arrested me for a 'public order' offence (without stating exactly what the offence was.)

The upshot being that I was lobbed in the back of the van and taken to a police station the other side of Manchester in Pendleton in Salford. And after spending ten hours (yes, TEN fucking hours!) in a cell I was interviewed and released on bail pending a decision by the Crown Prosecution Service as whether to proceed with charges or not.

At the end of the interview I was asked by one of coppers if there was anything I'd like to add and so I said yes, and said, "If that extract had been published in a national newspaper such as The Daily Mail or The Sun and a complaint was made, would you have gone and arrested the editors of those newspapers?"

They didn't answer. So I answered for them and said, "No, you wouldn't have. Would you?"

And it's true. They wouldn't have.

Likewise, if Joe's story was in a book that had been published by one of the big publishing houses such as Penguin Books or Harper Collins and a famous author had written the book would the police have gone and arrested the CEO's of Penguin Books and Harper Collins, and arrested the author?

Like fuck they would!

Yet because I'm a relatively unknown writer who self-publishes and I live in the area, the police come to my house, team handed, and arrest me.

Everyone I've spoken to about my arrest says the same thing - that it's a load of bollocks. And I wrote to the Crown Prosecution Service and told them exactly that.

This is part of the letter I wrote:

I was arrested on the above date and you're currently looking at whether to bring charges or not, and although you have my statement which I made to the police I also wish to provide you with further information for you to consider. Which, hopefully, after reading it, along with my statement, you'll agree that no charges should be brought against me.

I wasn't told what specific section of the public order offence it is that I was arrested for and I don't remember it being stated during the interview either, though I think I heard 'publication' being said prior to the interview commencing.

I've tried contacting the O.I.C (Officer In Charge) numerous times and left messages and sent emails asking him to contact me for clarification but I've received no reply. So I've had to Google what section I think it relates to and I think the section may possibly be publication of inflammatory material intending to stir up racial hatred and anti-immigrant feeling.

Apologies for repeating myself, as I've said some of this in my statement, but my arrest is a load of bollocks. Complete and utter fucking bollocks.

I'm also highly fucking pissed off and extremely annoyed about the manner in which I was arrested.

Having read the possession/publication part of the public order section on Google I'm guessing that your decision to bring charges is based on whether or not my intention was to stir up racial hatred and anti-immigrant feeling.

Well I can tell you now, it wasn't.

The only thing I intended to stir up was publicity for my book - like I've done countless times in the past using similar marketing methods in other areas (see enclosed marketing material.)

If I wanted to stir up racial tensions why the hell would I go to Hale - one of the poshest parts of Cheshire - to do it? What was I hoping that the wealthy, posh, well heeled, "nasty, vicious, middle aged thugs" of Hale do? Get tanked up on Dom Perignon in Piccolino's one lunch time and then charge around to the asylum seekers hotel and hit them with their Guggi handbags and spray Giorgio Armani perfume in their eyes?

It's pathetic. Absolutely fucking pathetic. And that woman who complained is pathetic too.

Like numerous people have commented on Facebook about her, some people really have got nothing better to do. Any normal person who got that flyer through their letter box and didn't agree with it would have just thought "what a load of shite" and flung it in the bin. Not run to the police with it.

And apart from the fact there wasn't any asylum seekers in Hale when I was posting the leaflets - and may not be if resident protest groups get their way - if I really wanted to stir up racial tensions I wouldn't go to Hale to do it would I? I'd go to one of the many inner city areas across England where racial tensions ARE high such as the area in

Sheffield that Joe mentions in his story where there are hundreds of immigrants already living there and distribute the flyer's there.

It's ludicrous - laughable even - to think that my intention was to stir up racial hatred. And I certainly wouldn't have received a letter off Prince William about the book in question if he or his advisors - who would have read the book to check through it - thought that I was in any way racist or if there was anything inciting racial hatred in it.

I also wouldn't receive messages and cards from black/mixed race premiership football managers like Chris Hughton wishing me good luck with my books if I was a racist would I? (copy enclosed.)

And if I thought for one minute that I might be committing an offence by distributing the flyers and there was a possibility that I could get arrested for stirring up racial hatred by doing so the last place I'd have sent one of the flyers would have been to Altrincham fucking police station! (see enclosed)...

As yet I've received no reply. (Altrincham police station covers Hale by the way.)

But what pissed me off, and really annoyed me, was the manner in which I was arrested.

I get arrested because some woman - who comes from a posh part of Cheshire - makes a ridiculous complaint about having a promotional leaflet for a book shoved through her letter box and the police act upon it immediately and send five coppers out within 24 hours to make an arrest and I get lobbed in the back of a police van and carted off to a police station eleven miles away and get locked in a cell for ten fucking hours.

Yet when someone like a pal of mine gets his house burgled in Stockport where I live - which *isn't* a posh area - like he did a couple of weeks previously and reported it to the police, it took the police EIGHT days to come out to investigate it.

And only two days before my arrest a builder at the top of my road had his van broken into and had over £3,000 worth of tools nicked out of it and when he rang the police they said it was 'only' a car crime and they wouldn't be sending anybody out and just gave him a crime reference number and told him to ring his insurance company.

What kind of policing is that? What's more serious; house burglary, car crime and theft in a working class area or a complaint about a flyer for a book being posted through the letter box of a house in an upper class area? Greater Manchester Police obviously think the latter.

No such thing as two-tier policing? Really...

It comes across as though the police have the attitude that if you're "well to do" and live in a posh area they'll investigate a crime for you - no matter how petty the complaint is. But if you're an 'ordinary Joe' (no pun intended, though Joe whose story it was is an ordinary bloke!) who lives in an ordinary suburb they *won't* investigate a crime for you, but they'll speedily rush to such an area, mob handed, to nick you for something. Even if it's a ridiculous - and false - accusation.

Furthermore, the police were quick to march through my front door to arrest me but when I tried contacting them to ask them to explain *exactly why* they marched through my front door they couldn't be arsed replying.

And the police wonder why they come in for so much stick?

Also, as I pointed out in my letter to the CPS, there's *no need* for me to stir up anti-immigrant feeling because the majority of Britain has ALREADY GOT anti-immigrant feeling. And the people of Hale have all got anti-immigrant feeling too otherwise they wouldn't be protesting about having asylum seekers and illegal immigrants being housed there!

As I've already said, my arrest really is a load of fucking bollocks. There was no need whatsoever for the police to turn up team handed at my house early on a Sunday morning. They could've just sent one, or maybe two coppers to ask my side of the story without arresting me and it could've all been cleared up.

It's a sad state of affairs when the police respond within a day to a complaint about a flyer but take over a week to respond to a house burglary - and just not respond at all to car crime.

But the saddest thing of all about my arrest was that it left my youngest daughter deeply disappointed. Not disappointed with *me* for getting arrested. She thought that was fucking hilarious! It was a *consequence* of my arrest that left her feeling disappointed. It also left me and my wife feeling disappointed for her too.

Me, my wife and my two daughters regularly go to Hale walking our dog. There's a restaurant in Hale Village, I forget the name of it now, and whenever we go my youngest says she'd like to go there one day. It's a bit out of my price bracket to be honest! However it was my daughter's 16th birthday at the end of January, three weeks after my arrest. And prior to my arrest, seeing as how sixteen is a 'special' birthday, I'd told her that we'd go there for her birthday which she was over the moon about. But we couldn't go because my bail conditions prevented me from going into Hale.

That's another reason why I was so pissed off and annoyed with my fucking pathetic arrest. An arrest that was instigated by a fucking pathetic old busybody.

But, as always, as those of you who have read my books know, I always try and see the funny side of things. And although I didn't think that my arrest was very funny there is a slightly humorous side to this story.

The night before I was arrested I was watching one of those twenty four hours in police custody type programmes and it showed the police smashing down the front door of a house and arresting the bloke whose house it was.

My youngest was sat watching it with me. She knows that I've got a bit of a 'chequered' past and that I've been in prison, and as the coppers handcuffed the bloke and put him in the back of the police van she jokingly said to me, "That's you dad!" So I laughed and said, "I don't think so. The days of *me* getting arrested are long gone."

Then fuck me, the following morning a load of coppers turn up at our house and arrest me!

And when I came back home later that night and walked in the front door my daughter came out of her bedroom, leant over the banister, and with a wry smile on her face said to me, "What was you saying about those days being long gone Dad?!"

An Ordinary Joe

During the Brexit debate, which turned into an utter fiasco and made the UK the laughing stock of Europe, I wrote what I suppose you could call an 'open letter' for everyone to read and I uploaded it to the internet. It was directed at those who were doing their utmost to stop Brexit, in the main, Jeremy Corbyn, Jo Swinson, Gina, Miller and Tony Blair.

I'm not massive into politics, I just felt like getting something off my chest. Some will agree with what I wrote, others won't. I don't really care to be honest. But I do care about what's happening to this country. And like millions of others, and like I put in my letter, I'm sick to death of immigrants flooding here - which was the reason people voted leave - and turning this country into a shit hole.

Right now, people who were born and bred in Britain and who have lived here all their lives and who have contributed to this country and paid all their taxes and national insurance contributions are struggling to pay for the basics.

They're struggling to buy food. They're struggling to clothe their kids. They're struggling to pay their gas and electric bills. They're struggling to pay their rent and mortgage. And thousands are relying on foodbanks. Whilst asylum seekers get it all for free and get put up in hotels.

It cost me and my family over £200 a night to stay in a hotel on a short break in London not so long ago. How much does it cost an asylum seeker to stay in a hotel? Nothing.

In fact, THEY GET PAID to stay in a hotel, £49.18 a week, each. Extra if they have children. Female asylum seekers also get a one off payment of £300 if they're expecting. (I don't recall my wife getting £300 payments for our two sons when they were born.) And they get fed three meals a day, plus free prescriptions, free dental care, and free eye tests (and free glasses if need be) whereas the likes of me and nearly every other British citizen has to pay for it.

Some councils are even giving asylum seekers free driving lessons and pay for their theory test and their driving test, and if they fail they'll pay for them to take it again. I had to pay £33 a lesson for my daughter's driving lessons and she had over thirty lessons, and she had to re-sit her theory test three times and re-take her driving test twice. All told it cost me over £1,300 to get her to pass her test yet asylum seekers get it for free.

Though asylum seekers don't really need to drive because in certain parts of the country they're entitled to free travel on buses and on trains. And they want to make it free for them to travel around London too on trains, buses and on the Underground. And not only can they get free travel, they get free prescriptions as well.

My wife is on life-long medication and each repeat prescription cost's just under a tenner. She's on four lots of medication and each time she goes to the chemist it costs her nearly forty quid and asylum seekers get their prescriptions for nothing. It's disgusting.

And this one really pissed me off.

About a year ago I had a tooth out which cost me £130. A friend of my wife's is the receptionist at our dentists and as I was sat chatting to her waiting to go in a youngish bloke about twenty years old who'd just been seen came back into reception. He was an asylum seeker. And he had an interpreter with him. The interpreter spoke to my wife's friend and they signed a few papers and left. And after they'd gone my wife's friend looked at me and shook her head and said, "Unbelievable."

And not only is this unbelievable, just like the likes of me and you have to pay anything between £30 to £40 for driving lessons and £10 for a prescription whilst asylum seekers and illegal immigrants get it for free, this too is disgusting.

It was a Monday morning when I went, having made the appointment ten days previously. The Friday before, this asylum seeker had spoken to whoever it is they speak to about issues they have saying he had toothache and they contacted the dentist for him and he was given an emergency appointment to have his tooth removed 48 hours later first thing on the Monday morning. He was prioritised, got treatment, and had his tooth taken out for free. Yet I had to pay £130.

It really is unbelievable. Some people struggle to even get registered at a dentists let alone get an appointment. And some have to travel miles out of their area to get registered with one. It really is taking the piss. And some hospitals guarantee to see asylum seekers within FIFTEEN minutes. One hospital even offers *failed* asylum seekers a free walk in service without having to provide documentation.

Old people - old *British* people - are dying in hospital corridors on make shift beds. And British people are having to wait up to seventeen hours in A&E to be seen by a doctor. But if you're an asylum seeker you can waltz into a hospital and be seen within a quarter of an hour.

Is it any wonder asylum seekers flock here in their thousands knowing what they can get? And they'll KEEP ON flocking here. And is it any wonder that millions of us are fed up and extremely fucking pissed off about it?

Official figures show that it costs nearly £45,000 a year to house just one asylum seeker - nearly a thousand pounds a week. And collectively the government are spending over £8 million pounds

A DAY putting asylum seekers up in hotels. That's over £3 billion pounds a year of tax payer's money being spent on illegal immigrants. And that's just on housing them in hotels. The *total* money spent on asylum seekers is in excess of FIVE billion a year.

How many hospitals could you build with that? And how many homeless people could you get off the streets? And how many new houses could you build with that amount of money? Though it'd be pointless spending it on building new houses because they'd probably just give them all to asylum seekers once they've been built. Just like they give them everything else.

Some families are worried sick about finances and money and are having to choose between 'heating or eating' - having the central heating on or cooking a meal - because they can't afford the two of them. Yet asylum seekers don't have to worry about that because they get both. For free. Neither do they have to worry about energy prices going up and increases in water and council tax bills like the rest of us do because it's all gets paid for them.

And the cheeky bastards STILL aren't happy.

You may have seen it on television not so long ago when about fifty of them camped in tents outside their hotel in London instead of sleeping in their rooms because they said the hotel wasn't good enough for them and demanded a better one. And at another hotel, that was originally a four star hotel before the asylum seekers moved in, they protested outside it with banners saying 'Homes Not Hotels.' One of them even went to see a solicitor to see if he could make a claim because he'd been the hotel for over eighteen months and it was "affecting his mental health."

I can't imagine for one minute that any homeless British citizen, of which there are thousands, would complain about being put up in a four star hotel free of charge. Three meals a day included.

Nor could I imagine them complaining that it affected their mental health. On the contrary. They'd be extremely grateful - unlike asylum seekers.

And it's equally bad in Ireland.

In Dublin, asylum seekers set up tent camps in Dublin city centre and along the Grand Canal. It was horrendous. It was like the migrant camps in Calais. It was a right eye sore. And just like we're sick to death of asylum seekers flocking here, so too are the people of Dublin and other parts of Ireland.

It was also reported that the government were considering scrapping free school meals for kids - kids who desperately need free school meals because their parents are struggling - because it was costing too much.

That's just one meal a day, for five days of the week, and for only thirty nine weeks of the year, school term(s). And the government say they can't afford it. Yet asylum seekers get THREE meals a day, SEVEN days a week, ALL YEAR ROUND. And the government happily pay for it. They probably give them a Christmas dinner on Christmas day too. (Not that many of them *celebrate* Christmas.) And it wouldn't surprise me if they gave them all party hats and a box of Christmas crackers as well.

We're the one's that are fucking crackers though.

Well, our government is. And feeding asylum seekers is obviously more of a priority for our government than feeding needy British kids.

And as for that headteacher at that school in Hampshire who cancelled Easter celebrations and cancelled the kids easter bonnet parade at the school - something which all kids love doing and look forward to - and are celebrating 'Refugee Week' instead, she should be sacked.

It's disgusting that she can get away with doing that. It's discrimination. We're a Christian country, though we won't be in a hundred years' time the way things are going, so what's wrong with celebrating a Christian festival?

It's people like her and the other "inclusivity and diversity" morons that cause all the friction. And is it any wonder again that people get wound up about it?

And some councils have also banned the word 'Christmas' in case it offends people and have told workers to use the phrase 'festive season' instead. They've also banned the sending of Christmas cards and no longer put up a Christmas tree. How bad - and pathetic - is that? And get this. If an asylum seeker or illegal immigrant, or any foreigner, was to say something to you in their native language and you couldn't understand them - which you're not going to - and you asked them to speak English you could be arrested for committing a 'hate crime'. How fucking ludicrous is that? Arrested. For asking someone to speak English. In England. When in Rome, as they say...

We really are losing our country. And identity. And I for one HATE those fucking left-wing arseholes who make these laws.

The worst thing that a lot of politicians did was oppose the Rwanda bill. Even royalty and the Church of England got in on the act to try and stop it. Prince Charles - or King Charles as he is now - said it was "appalling" that illegal immigrants should be deported to Rwanda. But how many immigrants has he got living on *his* street?

None, is the answer.

If he's so in favour of immigrants coming here why not put a few hundred up in Balmoral and

Sandringham and in the dozens of other royal residences that the royal family have around Britain? He could house thousands of them. (And he'd soon change his tune if he did and found out what it's like to have them living on his doorstep.)

The same goes for the Church of England.

Let immigrants stay in their churches if they care for them so much. The Church of England is worth millions. They too could easily afford to house a few thousand of them. Have they? No. But, as it's been widely reported on they'll happily baptise asylum seekers - the vast majority of which come from Muslim countries - converting them to Christianity in order for them to claim that they are at risk of persecution if they are deported back to their home country due to their 'new found' religion - a religion that most of them are opposed to and couldn't give a shit about.

And the same goes for those two-faced hypocritical 'Hope not Hate' and 'Refugees Welcome' protesters. How many of them have offered to house an immigrant? None of them. Well, apart from Gary Lineker that is. And the one that stayed at his house would've been handpicked too. It certainly wouldn't have been one that was plucked out of a dinghy off a beach in Dover that's for sure.

When these placard waving do-gooders see another boat full of (healthy fighting age male) asylum seekers arrive here do they actually think, "Oh, wonderful! More!"

Nonsense. It's all for show: "Look at *me*. How good am *I*, doing my bit."

But when they get the opportunity to do their bit, they won't.

Watch the YouTube video of the guy pretending to be from a refugee charity who asked fifty of the

'Hope Not Haters' at a protest would they be willing to house a refugee, having first 'drawn them in' by asking them about the kind of house they lived in and how many spare bedrooms they had.

Each one he asked said they had at least one spare bedroom, many had two, but not one of them said they'd be willing to accommodate a refugee. And when he asked them would they like to sponsor a refugee for £50, just a £1 a week, instead of housing one, they all said no thanks. And when he asked them would they be willing for a refugee to come to their house for a couple of hours each week for a 'chat and a cup of tea' to help them settle in and to make them feel welcome in Britain, guess what every single one of them said? No! Their excuses being that they "didn't really have the time."

Yet they've got plenty of time to spend at 'Anti Fascist' and 'Far Right' protests waving 'Refugees Welcome' placards.

Refugees Welcome? Don't make me laugh you hypocrites.

The majority of people thought the idea to send illegal immigrants to Rwanda was a good one. Help the genuine ones, yes. The one's that *really are* fleeing persecution and war. But get rid of the rest; the ones that are here for a free ride.

You've only got to look at the pictures in the newspapers and watch the news reports on television to see that nearly all the 'refugees' coming here who say that they are "scared for their lives" in their own country and are "fleeing persecution" are fit and healthy young males aged around 18 - 25. Very few are women, kids or the elderly. These 'refugees' are liars. They are *not* fleeing persecution. And they are *not* genuine refugees. And anyone who believes that they are - King Charles and the leaders of the Church of England included (and football pundits) - are fucking idiots.

You don't see many fit and healthy 18 - 25 year old Ukrainian males trying to sneak into Britain do you? That's because they've decided to stay and fight for their country, a fight which is against one of the most powerful armies in the world, Russia. Unlike those seeking refuge in our country who all they are 'supposedly' fleeing are rag tag bands of rebels and half-baked piss pot armies.

One other thing that amazes me about these "poor helpless refugees" who sneak into our country is that on the way here they always seem to lose their passports and ID papers and anything else that may reveal their identity, their (true) age, their origin and so on. But they never lose their mobile phones do they? Isn't that amazing?

Those who try and cross the channel in dinghies and small boats know the risks, so if they drown trying to get here it's their own fault and they've got no-one to blame but themselves. If you cross a busy main road when the lights are on green instead of waiting for them to turn red and you get knocked down it's your own fault isn't it? And the same goes for illegal immigrants. They're not being forced at gunpoint to get in those boats are they?

I've got no sympathy for them. And I'm not alone either. Many others think the same way.

There was a group of us talking about the immigration problem/Rwanda plan in our local pub not so long ago - a pub that's not far from an area in Sheffield that's blighted by immigrants - and one bloke in our company said that when he sees on television that a boat has capsized in the English Channel and immigrants have drowned he doesn't think, "Oh, how sad." He said he thinks, "Good. I hope more boats capsize."

A couple of years ago the brother of an illegal immigrant who drowned in the channel was interviewed on television and he actually said that his brother wasn't in any danger in the country where he lived and that he was only coming to England because he wanted a better life. (And quite unbelievably his family and the other families of those who drowned tried to sue UK Coastguards saying it was their fault.)

Well I wouldn't mind a better life myself. And I dare say that millions of other British people wouldn't mind a better life as well.

I wouldn't mind going to live in Spain. And if I drowned in the Med' off the coast of Benidorm trying to get there would I, or my family, get any sympathy off the Spanish people? No. I wouldn't.

And if I made it to Spain would I be allowed to stay there? Again. No, I wouldn't. I'd be sent back. Just like the illegal immigrants who try to get into our country should be sent back - or sent to Rwanda.

And that's the key word: ILLEGAL.

If you do something that's illegal you're breaking the law - you're committing a criminal act. (And a lot of the immigrants ARE criminals, coming from places like Albania where there is no war or persecution. In actual fact Albania is a popular holiday destination.) And if a UK Citizen like myself were to break the law and commit criminal acts would I be rewarded for doing so by being put up in a cushy hotel and given three meals a day and have all my bills paid for AND be given nearly a £50 a week spending allowance? (And free driving lessons.) No, I certainly wouldn't. I'd be flung in a police cell.

Some people, i.e. out of touch MP's and those who have no immigration problem in the 'nice' areas where they live, have got no idea of just how much the majority of the UK resent illegal immigrants.

And just because people protest about immigration it doesn't make us racists or fascists or 'Far Right' as we're branded. We're just fed up with immigrants flooding here and claiming benefits, free housing, free health care and anything else they can get their hands on whilst some of our own citizens - some of whom have fought for this country - get nothing and are left homeless and are forced to beg on the streets.

It's not right. Or fair.

The answer to stopping illegal immigrants coming here by the way is simple: give them nothing when they get here. Obviously preventing them from getting here in the first place is the best way to do it (and giving £millions of pounds to African countries to try and stop it like the government are doing isn't the answer) but if they do get here, give them sod all.

Ex-servicemen who have fought for this country and who are now sleeping rough on the streets are given sod all so why give an illegal immigrant anything?

Like I say, nearly all of those who come here aren't in danger or in fear for their lives in the country they've "escaped" from like they claim they are. They just use that as an excuse.

But let's assume that *is* the reason for them fleeing their country. If so, once they've escaped their own country to a neighbouring country they've achieved their objective haven't they? They're safe.

Take Somalian's for example. Once they've made it to neighbouring Kenya or Ethiopia they're safe. So why do they then feel the need to travel all the way across Africa and through another half a dozen countries in Europe and then camp out in squalor in France for six months whilst trying to smuggle into the UK to be safe?

There's no need. Because they were safe in Kenya or Ethiopia. And the reason they come - and will *keep on* coming - is because we are far too soft. Or rather, our government is far too soft. And the asylum seekers and the illegal immigrants know we'll let them in. And until we *stop letting them in* they'll keep on coming. In droves.

If you feed a stray dog it'll keep coming back. Stop feeding it and it'll stop coming.

This country is turning into a right shit hole. There are towns and cities here that are more reminiscent of third world countries than they are of England. And as for those hypocritical halfwits that stand there waving their placards with 'Refugees Welcome' written on them at demonstrations, what I suggest is to take around two thousand asylum seekers and illegal immigrants and dump them in THEIR town. Put them on THEIR street. Put them in the houses next door to THEM. Put them in the houses opposite them. Put them in the flats above and below them. Have them hang around the street corners on THEIR high street. Have them drive around THEIR streets in clapped out transit vans (that probably aren't even insured) early in the morning pinching all the charity clothing bags.

And then every Saturday and Sunday allow them all to gather in gangs in THEIR city centre in pockets of Somalians, Afghans, Eastern Europeans, etc, making shoppers and families feel very uneasy - uneasy in their own country - and see how THEY like it (and stick a few hundred on Gary Lineker's street.)

And if you *did do that* you can guarantee that at the next demonstration those idiots will have added the word 'NOT' on their placards in-between the words Refugees and Welcome.

You don't see it as much now because the camps in Calais have gone. But those 'poor' 18 - 25 year old males who have 'fled' their country claiming they are scared for their lives living there and have fled for fear of being attacked, or to escape the fighting weren't scared to attack British lorry drivers like they did were they when trying to hide in the back of their lorries?

Neither are they scared to have pitch battles with the French police. And they also have no fear of fighting each other with knives and machetes in gang feuds in the camps like it's been shown on television they do. And so if they're capable of doing things like that then they are more than capable of fending for themselves in their own country.

I once read an article in the newspaper and in it a Labour MP said how immigration "painted a delightful picture of multicultural Britain."

Delightful? What planet is he on? It might be delightful where *he* lives but it's certainly not delightful for a lot of people in many towns and cities across the UK. Including *my* town.

Maybe that MP should move to one district in Sheffield not far from where I live where it's overrun with Romanian Gypsies and which has been described as a "time bomb waiting to explode" by the local press and see if it's delightful to live there. As he'll soon discover, and as residents there know, it's *far* from delightful.

Or perhaps he could go and live in a part of Oldham for a week or two that was in the papers not so long ago and see how delightful it is to live there. But then again he wouldn't *be able* to live there because as everyone knows it's a no-go area unless you're of a 'particular' ethnicity.

Keir Starmer promised to "smash the smuggling gangs" and "massively reduce" the amount of illegal immigrants coming here. But what has he done about it since becoming Prime Minister?

Nothing at all is the answer. In actual fact it's *got worse* since he became Prime Minister.

And if he doesn't get the immigration crisis - and it IS a crisis, a huge one - under control he won't have a cat in hells chance of being re-elected at the next general election. Nigel Farage and Reform will walk it. And that's where my vote will be going. As will thousands of other people's.

People slag Farage off but I'd rather have him as our prime minister than that useless wanker we've got now.

This 'delightful' country is going down the pan. It's an absolute joke. Only the joke isn't funny anymore and no-one's laughing. Well, apart from the refugees, asylum seekers and the illegal immigrants who come here that is.

They think it's absolutely hilarious and they're laughing like hyenas. At us.

***

The Crown Prosecution Service have since told the police that no charges should be brought. And rightly so. Many thanks to Billy Graham for allowing his story to be told and for extracts from his books to be reproduced. Those books were:

52

My Dad's A Dickhead

By Billy Graham

The first time I was sent to jail I took it really badly. I refused to eat or drink. I lashed out and spat and swore at anyone who came near me. I threw chairs and tables around the room. I even smeared my own faeces all over the walls. After that we never played Monopoly ever again in our house!

I was driving down the road the other day with my wife and my two kids and there was a bin lorry in front of us and all of a sudden this huge dildo fell out of the back of it and bounced off the windscreen and the kids shouted, "WOW! What was that Dad?" Embarrassed, and not wanting to tell them what it really was, I said, "It was just a flying insect." To which my youngest replied, "Was it? I'm surprised it could get off the fucking ground with a cock that big!"

They were just jokes, obviously! Which relate to stories in the book. Though Billy *has* been in prison. And a huge dildo didn't really fall out of the back of a bin lorry and bounce off Billy's windscreen as he was driving behind it with his wife and kids. And his youngest didn't say that either. Though if Billy *was* driving behind a bin lorry with his wife and kids and a huge dildo fell out of the back of it and bounced off the windscreen Billy's youngest *probably would* come out with something like that! And that's because the apple never falls far from the tree.

All kids think their dads are dickheads. They don't think it all the time but there'll be occasions when they do. Billy Graham was no exception. And he too often thought the same thing about *his* dad. But what Billy didn't realise was that 'dad dickheadedness' can be hereditary and can be passed from father to son. And similar to how Billy used to look at HIS dad and think "what a dickhead," Billy's kids now look at HIM and think the same thing!

Though there's one difference. Billy learnt from his dad's mistakes.

Like a lot of father and son relationships can sometimes be, Billy didn't always see eye to eye with his dad. His dad was 'old school' and had the "do as I say not as I do" attitude, an attitude that Billy thinks is the wrong one to have with your kids. Like he says, if your kids copy something you do and you tell them off for doing it they're going to think, "Well *you* do it so why can't I!"

Billy's upbringing was tough. And it was made even tougher by his dad's alcohol addiction. An addiction that resulted in tearing Billy's family apart. And coupled with the mental health issues that his dad suffered with, his dad's alcohol addiction eventually resulted in his dad committing suicide. So it's little wonder that Billy went off the rails in life and at one point ended up in prison.

But he learnt from that mistake too.

Billy was a proper jack the lad. He was THE lad. And he was *going to continue* being the lad. Because "marriage, kids, and a mortgage - and all that bollocks!" as he put it, wasn't for him. But little did he know that his life was about to change - for the better. And fortunately, having learnt from his mistakes, he didn't make the mistake of *not* getting married. And he went from jack the lad to Billy the dad! And he realised that marriage and kids was *exactly* for him. Though he could've done without the mortgage! Like we all could!

Not many dads have led the kind of life that Billy has led. Not many would want to either! And very few dads have done the things that Billy has done - and lived to tell the tale. (Quite literally.)

His story is compelling, captivating, touching and heart-warming. And absolutely hilarious! And the valuable lessons Billy has learnt in life have ensured that the two apples that have fallen from his tree have had the kind of upbringing that all kids should have; a happy, fun filled one. With a dad that's a right dickhead!

Gangsters Goons And Raving Loons

(And Bent Coppers And The Devious And Underhanded Tactics The Police Use)

By Billy Graham

During a discussion at school about what parents did for a living the teacher asked one boy what his dad's job was and the lad said, "My Dad runs the local fire station. He's the station officer." The teacher said, "That's excellent Simon. Your Dad's got a very responsible job."

The teacher then asked the boy sat next to him what his dad did and the boy said, "My dad drives an ambulance. He's in charge of the local ambulance service." And the teacher said, "That's fantastic Bobby. Well done."

The teacher then asked another boy what his dad did and the boy replied, "My dad runs the local prison." And the teacher said, "Excellent, Johnny!

Is he the prison governor?" And Johnny said, "No Miss - he's the hardest cunt in there!"

In 1983 singer Frankie Vaughan released the song 'Stockport' which included the line "I'm going back to Stockport. It's the place for me." A lot has happened in the town since that song was recorded and considering that Stockport was recently listed as one of the top ten most dangerous towns in England to live for assault, murder, muggings, drug dealing and violent crime, if Frankie Vaughan was still alive and he re-recorded that song today he may well change the line from, "I'm going back to Stockport" to "Fuck that! I'm never stepping foot in the town ever again!"

Someone else who probably wouldn't rush back there if they were still alive is David Bowie. Because a little known - and amusing fact - is that after Bowie performed at the famous Poco Poco nightclub in the town in 1970, whilst waiting for his train back home to London he fell asleep on a bench at Edgeley station and someone nicked his wallet! Only in Stockport!!

From famous celebrities, premiership footballers and real housewives, to notorious underworld figures, corrupt coppers and real hardmen, you could say Stockport's got the lot. It's also home to Angela Rayner, the deputy prime minister. Who might get a bit of a shock if she reads the book and realises what's been going on in her hometown over the years!

The book will be a right eye opener for many. And if you're thinking, "I've never been to Stockport so there's no point in me buying it because I won't appreciate it." Think again. If you've got a broad sense of humour (and aren't easily shocked) it won't matter WHERE you're from. You WILL appreciate it. Though you probably won't add Stockport to your bucket list of places to visit after you've read it!

Imagine Lock Stock And Two Smoking Barrels, The Sweeney, Minder, Snatch, The Krays, and the books Hard Bastards, Gangland, and the Guv'nor all rolled into one. With Borat and The Inbetweeners causing chaos in the middle of it all! And that's what this book is.

Those featured in the stories include Lenny McLean, Roy Shaw, Lee Duffy, Paul Massey, Billy Isaacs, Chris Little, The Quality Street Gang, Jimmy Swords, Arthur Donnelly, 'Jimmy the Weed' Donnelly, John Fury, Tyson Fury, The 'Teflon Don' and The Kray's associate Ronnie Field. Angela Rayner's boss 'two-tier Keir' gets a mention (slagged off!) too. And if you think there's no such thing as two-tier policing one story about Greater Manchester Police will make you think again.

Stars including Will Mellor, Michelle Keegan, Ricky Hatton, Danny Miller, Craig Cash, Tess Daly, Yvette Fielding, Phil Foden, Lee Boardman and Jason Manford who all come from Stockport also feature. (Jason Manford is from Salford but regards Stockport as his home.) There are also stories about Alex Higgins, Jimmy White, Gary Lineker and Kenny Dalglish.

And details of the lies that the police deliberately spread and had published by the media in order to save face after "bottling it" and "giving in" to an infamous Manchester gangster are also revealed. As are details of alleged police involvement in the gangster's murder two years later. It also includes the story Sticks And Stones Will Break Your Bones But Concrete Lintels Do A Far Better Job by a notorious gangland figure who gives a frightening insight into what can happen if you cross the wrong the people in Britain's underworld.

So why not put your feet up (unlike the fella in the sticks and stones story you'll still be able to walk when you put them back down again!) and enjoy a 'gangster' book like no other. A book that during the writing of, several people were shot, stabbed, murdered, impaled with crossbows, had their legs snapped in half with concrete lintels and were battered senseless with fifteen inch rubber dildos! And one poor bloke nearly had his cock torn off with a pair of pliers! And it's all in the book!

Foreword by London Gangster Dave Courtney (R.I.P.)

*A script for a television comedy/comedy drama based on Billy's books is now being written.

You may also like these similar books by one of our other authors, Adam Gleeson...

Awfully Funny

By Adam Gleeson

Dementia is an awful disease, and if a loved one of yours has suffered from it or one of your loved one's *is* suffering from it then you'll know just how awful it is. But as distressing and as upsetting as it can be, not just for the person who has got it but for every other member of the family too, every now and then there can be some funny moments, which can either be something the person who is suffering from it says or something they do.

Adam Gleeson cared for his mum when she had dementia, and as well as the many heartbreaking moments there were also several humorous moments. And after his mum died a friend of his suggested he write a book about the funny things that often occur whilst looking after someone with dementia.

At first Adam was slightly reluctant to do it as he thought that it might be a bit 'cruel' to laugh about such things. But as his friend said, you're not laughing at the person- be it your mum, dad, husband or wife who is suffering from it - you're laughing at what it is they've done. And chances are that the person who has done 'the daft thing' would probably laugh themselves if they knew they'd done it.

Adam's mum would have *definitely* laughed if she'd have known that some of the things she was doing were so stupid! And so with that in mind Adam decided to do it and he got people to send him their stories to put alongside his own, and the stories are guaranteed to bring a smile to the face of anyone who has ever had a loved one suffer from dementia. And not only will they bring a smile to your face they'll have you holding your sides laughing!

One of those who contributed stories sums dementia up when he describes it as a thief that comes in the night and steals memories and thoughts from the mind, and it keeps coming back every night stealing more and more memories and thoughts until they've all gone. And then once the thief has left and taken all of the person's memories with them a demon starts coming and starts planting bad and unpleasant thoughts in their mind. The bad thoughts then start to take over and gradually wear the person's brain down until it eventually stops working.

It also wears the person's loved one's down too. And it's equally bad for them watching it happen. It can be worse in fact. Because a loved one can see the thief and the demon at work but there's absolutely nothing they can do to stop them. All they can do is watch. And suffer. Just like their mum, dad, husband or wife is suffering.

As Adam says, "I've seen and done things that no son should have to see or do for their mum. And I won't be the only one. There'll be thousands of other sons - and daughters - who have to do things for their mum's and dad's that they really shouldn't have to. But we do those things because we don't forget the things that our mum's and dad's did for us. I've seen it all with my mum, from the hilarious and the comical to the tragic, the despairing and the pitiful. I even thought about killing my mum to put her out of her misery. So if a loved one of yours suffers from dementia, when funny and humorous moments come along make the most of them, because for every funny and humorous moment there'll be a thousand awful ones."

Adam's book is heartrending, tear-jerking and extremely moving. But, as awful as dementia is, as the stories in it show, at times it can be *awfully funny*.

It's A Mad Bad Funny And Sad
(And Very Dangerous) World We Live In

Extraordinary Stories By Ordinary People

By Adam Gleeson

Imagine being woken up in the middle of the night by an 'itchy' feeling at the top of your leg and when you scratch it you can't feel yourself scratching, and no matter how hard you scratch you still can't feel yourself scratching your leg. Then when you look down you realise why. *You're not scratching your leg.* You're scratching the head of an 18ft python that's swallowing you alive and has swallowed you right up to your hips.

Imagine being a thirteen year old boy and you come home from school and your dad asks you to go to the shop to get some flowers for your mum and when you come back you find your dad hanging at the top of the stairs with a rope around his neck. Dead. Having hung himself knowing that you'd be the one that would find him. And if you were happily married with three great kids and you were successful, with a good job and had no worries in life, what could cause you to feel totally worthless and useless to anybody and make you feel so low that it forces you into bouts of deep depression that are absolute torture and that you struggle to get out of? These two stories give an insight into what it's like to suffer with your mental health.

Imagine walking into Harrods and spending £65,000 on a sofa, £3,000 on a rug, £7,000 on a coffee table (that you put on top of your £3,000 rug!) £15,000 on a bed and £4,000 on baubles for the Christmas tree! And you give your wife a £70,000 a year handbag allowance. Welcome to the world of the super-rich.

Imagine being forced to watch as a loved one is shot dead in front of you and then two weeks after burying them you open your front door one morning and see their corpse propped up against a wall outside your house. It'd be pretty horrific wouldn't it? Now imagine how it must feel to be forced to watch not just *one* loved one being shot dead in front of you but being forced to watch as every single member of your family - including your wife, your kids, your grandkids and your mum and dad - are shot dead in front of you, and then seeing ALL their corpses propped up against a wall outside your house when you open your front door one morning. Well that's what can happen if you cross the Mexican Drug Cartels.

And can dogs really sense danger and know when something bad is going to happen like it's said they can? One woman who was sceptical they could now think's differently after her dogs began howling and wailing one night seconds before her husband was killed in a road traffic accident.

And parents often say that if anyone ever harmed their kids they'd kill the person responsible and make them suffer. Though in reality most parents wouldn't do it. But one parent *did* do it. And not only did he make the perpetrator suffer he made him *suffocate*. By burying him alive.

And you'd think that Cancer Research UK would be grateful for ANY donations wouldn't you? Not so. As one man found out when CRUK turned his donation down. (It's all about "image" apparently. Strange that. Because we, like everyone else, thought it was all about raising money to find a cure for a horrible disease.) And *will* one in two of us - half the world - really get cancer like CRUK claim? Or are they just scaremongering? You can make your own mind up after reading this shocking story and the statistics that go with it.

And would you be able to keep a straight face if you worked on reception at A&E in your local hospital and a half naked man hobbled in with a cucumber wedged in his anus and when you asked him how it got there he said that he was making a salad in the nude and dropped the cucumber and slipped and fell on it and it got stuck up his bum!

We live in a world that's full of lame excuses too!

From the frightening to the fascinating to the wonderful and the weird, and from the horrific to the hilarious to the heartbreaking and the inhumane, if you like extraordinary true life stories this is the book for you.

Can You Spare A Multi Millionaire A Pound Please

By Adam Gleeson

If a tramp asked you if you could spare him a cigarette and after you kindly gave him one he took £200 out of his pocket and gave it to you what would you think? Or if you saw a homeless man sat in a shop doorway and you gave him a bit of loose change and he got up and gave you a handful of £20 notes how would you react? And imagine just how elated you'd feel if you were up to your eye balls in debt and were about to be evicted from your home and a Good Samaritan came along and cleared your rent arrears for you and paid off all your debts and then paid for you and your two kids to go to Disney World in Florida. Well those scenarios - and dozens more like them - have actually happened. And the 'tramp' and the 'homeless man' and the Good Samaritan are one and the same person.

Whilst driving his car one day, Adam Gleeson pulled onto a pay and display car park and as he walked towards the machine to get a ticket he noticed a man sat in a Bentley Continental, a car that was worth around £150,000, parked in the bay next to the machine. And as Adam was getting his ticket the man got out of the Bentley and asked him could he spare him a £1 so he too could get a ticket. Adam started laughing and jokingly said to the man, "Are you taking the mickey?! You're driving a car like that and you're asking me for a pound!"

The man explained that he'd left his house without his wallet and didn't have any change for a ticket and so Adam thought well it's something we've all done, left the house without any money, and he gave the man a pound coin so he could get a car parking ticket. And the man thanked him. Put his hand in his pocket. Took two £50 notes out. Gave them to Adam - along with his £1 coin back - and got in his Bentley and drove off!

It transpired that Adam had just past one of Tom's - the driver of the Bentley - kindness tests that he sometimes does where he rewards people for showing kindness towards others. It also transpired that Tom was a multi-millionaire worth in excess of £100 million and who one day realised that he'd never get around to spending all the money he's got, so he started giving it away - to complete strangers in bizarre and unusual ways, leaving them totally bewildered into the bargain.

From sending hundreds of pounds inside Christmas cards to people he's never met, to hiding wads of cash inside newspapers on the London Underground for people to find and leaving it hanging out of cash dispensers for people to take, to clearing a single mum's debts and paying for her and her two young daughters to go on a dream holiday to Disney World in Florida which totalled over £10,000, to taking another family he'd never met before out on his yacht for the day in Majorca and then paying for their holiday too, which amounted to over £5,000. He's also put a homeless man up in a hotel in Brighton for a week and thrown $100 dollar bills (the equivalent of a week's wage) out of his hotel window in Thailand to local Thai people on the street below!

Tom also tells of why he once gave a woman in Tesco's a £100 because she sneezed, carried a nurse's shopping to her car for her and then gave her £250, bought an elderly couple an expensive plasma television in Curry's, how he goes into shops and hides money inside clothes and books for people to find when they buy them and take them home, why he paid for fifty people's MOT's at a garage, and how he asked a road sweeper if he believed in the saying 'where there's muck there's money' and then watched as he dived into his own litter bin after he told him he'd just thrown a thousand pounds in it!

Bizarre? Slightly Odd? Maybe. Does Tom's generosity brighten up people's day and put a smile on their faces? Definitely. And to Tom that's all that matters. And it's one of the most remarkable stories you'll ever read.

Also available...

Not All Husbands Are Annoying – Some Are Dead

By Ruth Jennings

I remember WHERE I married my husband and I remember WHEN I married my husband. I just can't remember WHY I married him.

I was at a boxing match not so long ago and one of the boxers got knocked out in the first round and my husband said to me, "That was boring, it was all over in less than a minute." So I said to him, "Now you know how I feel when we have sex."

A wife was arguing with her husband about their sex life and the husband says, "When you die I'm getting a headstone that reads Here Lies My Wife - As Cold As Ever." And his wife replies, "And when YOU die I'm getting a headstone that reads, Here Lies My Husband - Stiff At Last."

Three words that will shatter your husband's ego: Is it in?

My friend said to me, "My husband left me the other day, I've tried crying but tears just won't come out. What can I do to make myself cry?" So I said, "Imagine he's come back again."

What do toilets, birthdays and anniversaries have in common? Husbands miss them all.

A woman went to the doctors to get her husband's blood test results and the receptionist said to her, "We'll need a urine sample, a stool sample and a sample of your husband's semen." So the woman said, "I'll drop a pair of his underpants off tomorrow."

My husband was in the kitchen cooking my breakfast for me last Sunday when all of a sudden I heard a loud thud. So I ran in and found him lying collapsed unconscious on the floor, blue in the face and not breathing. I panicked at first and didn't know what to do and I started to get really worried. Then I remembered...

Wetherspoons do an all day breakfast for just £4.99

Ruth Jennings was happily married for ten years. Ten out of thirty isn't bad! She's now happily divorced and to celebrate she's released this book which is crammed full of jokes about husbands and marriage. And if you're married, or divorced like Ruth is, you'll find it absolutely hilarious. It'll also make an ideal gift for 'Hubby'. Though don't be surprised if your husband files for divorce after he's read it!

Three Vaginas And A Permanent Erection

Silly Facts, Silly Questions, and Silly Answers

By Asilic Unt

Did you know that you can tell the sex of a horse by counting its teeth? Although it's much easier to just look underneath and see if there's a massive cock swinging around!

Did you know that semen is ejaculated faster than Usain Bolt can run?

Did you know that a pigeon sees more frames per second than human beings do which gives them more time to asses danger and so only move if they have to. Which could explain why they leave it until the very last second before flying out of the way (causing you to think you've ran it over and squashed it) when you're driving towards one that's nonchalantly sat in the middle of the road!

And did you know that contrary to what many people believed there never were any characters called Seaman Staines, Master Bates, and Roger The Cabin Boy in the 1970's kids cartoon series Captain Pugwash. That said, in the Urban Dictionary, Pugwash is defined as "Cum that drains out of the anus after anal intercourse."

And to think we used to sit there eating our tea whilst we watched that as well!

Got a broad sense of humour? Like amusing funny facts? Then you'll like this book!

All of our books are available on Amazon

And thank you for buying this one

Printed in Great Britain
by Amazon